Language Development A

with Standardized Test Pra

2

Scott Foresman

Accelerating English Language Learning

Authors

Anna Uhl Chamot
Jim Cummins
Carolyn Kessler
J. Michael O'Malley
Lily Wong Fillmore

Consultant

George González

ISBN 0-13-028542-0

Pearson Education
10 Bank Street, White Plains, NY 10606

45678910—CRK—0504030201

Contents

Groups of People

Draw lines to match the pictures to the words.

1. friends

2. family

3. team

What can these groups do?

Fill in the blanks with action words.

1. Members of a chorus _____ together.

2. Team members _____ games together.

3. Family members _____ things.

4. Neighbors _____ each other.

5. Friends _____ together.

6. Class members _____ things together.

Name _____

What's wrong with this picture?

Circle the things that do not belong in your community.

Where do you go?

Use these words to fill in the blanks.

bakery	grocery store	library
park	post office	school

1. I want to buy cake.

   _____

   I go to the _____ .

2. I want to play.

   _____

   I go to the _____ .

3. I want to mail a package.

   _____

   I go to the _____ .

4. I want to buy food.

   _____

   I go to the _____ .

5. I want to learn English.

   _____

   I go to _____ .

6. I want to get a book.

   _____

   I go to the _____ .

Special Places

Names of special places start with a capital letter.

ABCDEFGHIJKLMNOPQRSTUVWXYZ.

1. Write the name of the state where you live.

_____

- - - - - - - - - - - - - - - - - - - -

_____

2. Write the name of this country.

_____

- - - - - - - - - - - - - - - - - - - -

_____

3. Write the name of your school.

_____

- - - - - - - - - - - - - - - - - - - -

_____

4. Write the name of your city.

_____

- - - - - - - - - - - - - - - - - - - -

_____

Time for a Rhyme

Circle the word to make the two lines rhyme.

1. I went out for a walk today.
   My neighborhood she looked _____ .   happy   okay

2. My grandmother was lifting weights,
   And dishwashers were juggling _____ .   plates   cups

3. The dentist shaved someone's head.
   The baker was baking sweet-tooth _____ .   cake   bread

Name _____

Tell what you like.

Circle the sentences that tell about someone liking something.

1. "My house is special," said the girl.

2. Grown-ups don't like to line up for recess.

3. "My school is great," said the boy.

4. The man did not want his head shaved.

5. Red is my favorite color.

6. I love to eat apples.

7. I like to see my friends.

8. The dogs like to wave at the cats.

Work with a partner. Write a sentence showing you like something.
Use the sentences above for help.

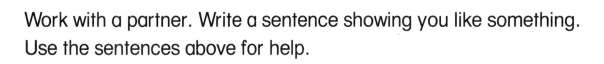

People or Places?

Use these words to complete the word webs below.

class	team	family	school
friends	bakery	park	library

People

Places

Name _____

Reading Objective:
Recall supporting ideas and details.

Sample:

The bakery in Rosa's neighborhood is a great place. Rosa and her mother go there on Saturdays. They see many kinds of food that they like to eat. There are cakes. There are cookies. There are rolls and many kinds of bread. Rosa loves to smell the bread that comes out of the oven. The smell makes her hungry. The baker's name is Mrs. Garcia. She is a friendly woman. She helps Rosa and her mother. Rosa and her mother tell Mrs. Garcia what they want to buy. She gives them the food. Then they go home and eat.

1. Why is the bakery a great place?

○ It is in the neighborhood.
○ Rosa and her mother go there.
○ It has food that they like to eat and smell.
The best choice: It has food that they like to eat and smell.

2. What did Rosa and her mother see?

○ many people walking down the street
○ cakes, cookies, rolls, and bread
○ a fruit market
The best choice: cakes, cookies, rolls, and bread

Try It

Read each question. Then read the story summary. Answer each question.

The neighborhood in <u>My Perfect Neighborhood</u> is a strange place. When the girl walks around her neighborhood, she sees many strange things.

Animals do the same actions that people do. Dogs wave at cats. Birds play drums. Poodles wear wedding dresses. People do strange things too.

Builders make buildings that look like pies. Grown-ups wait outside the school to play. Dishwashers juggle dishes.

The girl loves her walks. She likes to see what people and animals do.

1. Why is the neighborhood a strange place?

   ○ The girl walks around her neighborhood.

   ○ There are dogs, cats, and birds.

   ○ Animals and people do strange things.

2. What is a strange thing that animals do?

   ○ Builders cover buildings with food.

   ○ Poodles wear wedding dresses.

   ○ Cats go to many places in the neighborhood.

Which one does not belong?

Circle the animal that does not belong.

1. These animals live in the water.

2. These animals have six legs.

3. These animals have feathers.

4. These animals have hair or fur.

Has or Have?

Write **has** or **have** on the line.

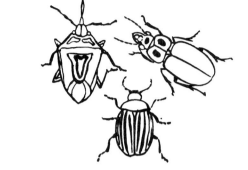

1. Insects _____ six legs.

2. A butterfly _____ six legs.

3. Mammals _____ hair or fur.

4. A lion _____ hair or fur.

5. A dog _____ hair or fur.

Name _____

Short a

Listen as your teacher names the pictures.
Circle the pictures whose names have the short *a* sound.

1.

2.

3.

4.

5.

6.

Animal Match

1. Draw a line to match each animal with its habitat.

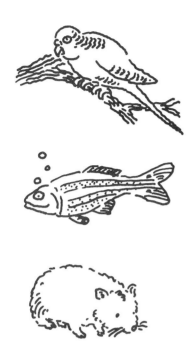

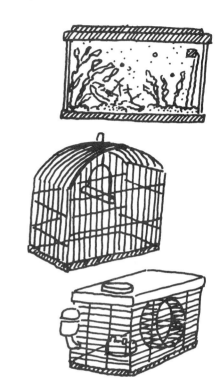

2. Draw a line to match each animal with its food.

Animals, Animals

Write the names of animals.
List the name under the correct heading.

Fish	Birds	Insects	Mammals

Look at the animal names in your chart.

How many are fish? _____

How many are birds? _____

How many are insects? _____

How many are mammals? _____

I Am . . .

Use animal names to fill in the blanks.

_____
- -

1. I am as smart as a _____.

_____
- -

2. I am as funny as a _____.

_____
- -

3. I am as friendly as a _____.

_____
- -

4. I am as happy as a _____.

Rhyme Time

Listen to your teacher say the words.
Circle the word that rhymes with the first word.

1. **air**   cold   bear   fuzzy

2. **nice**   nap   swimmer   ice

3. **cat**   fur   fat   clean

4. **log**   pond   green   frog

Animal Bingo

Cover the animal your teacher names.

Name _____

Math Objective: Find missing items in patterns.

Sample:

UP ⟶ ADD   DOWN ⟵ SUBTRACT

⟶

0 1 2 3 4 5 6 7 8 9 10   0 1 2 3 4 5 6 7 8 9 10

⟵

Look at the number lines. Look at these number patterns.
What is the next number in this pattern?

2, 4, 6, 8, _____

If you chose 10, you are right.

We are **adding** 2 each time, so the next number is 10.

$8+2=10$

What is the next number in this pattern?

8, 6, 4, _____

If you chose 2, you are right.

We are **subtracting** 2 each time, so the next number is 2.

$4-2=2$

Name _____

Try It

Look at the number lines. Choose only 1 answer for each question.

UP ⟶ ADD

0 1 2 3 4 5 6 7 8 9 10

DOWN ⟵ SUBTRACT

0 1 2 3 4 5 6 7 8 9 10

1. Find the next number in the number pattern:

   1, 3, 5, 7, _____

   ○ 6   ○ 8

   ○ 9   ○ 4

2. Find the next number in the number pattern:

   1, 4, 7, _____

   ○ 0   ○ 8

   ○ 9   ○ 10

3. Find the next number in the number pattern:

   9, 7, 5, _____

   ○ 3   ○ 8

   ○ 4   ○ 6

4. Find the next number in the number pattern:

   10, 6, _____

   ○ 2   ○ 3

   ○ 8   ○ 4

Who helps us?

Write the name of the worker.

police officer

crossing guard

firefighter

nurse

teacher

_____

1. A _____ helps make us well.

2. My _____ teaches us English.

3. A _____ puts out fires.

4. A _____ helps us cross the street.

5. A _____ helps keep us safe.

Name _____

People at Work

Look at the action words in the box.
Write the word that finishes each sentence.

collect	find
deliver	help

_____

1. Garbage collectors _____ garbage.

_____

2. Paramedics _____ people who are hurt.

_____

3. Librarians help us _____ books.

_____

4. Mail carriers _____ mail.

Where do I work?

Write the place where each worker works.

bank

factory

farm

office

1. I am a factory worker.

   _____
   - - - - - - - - - - - - - - - - -
   I work in a _____.

2. I am a farmer.

   _____
   - - - - - - - - - - - - - - - -
   I work on a _____.

3. I am a bank teller.

   _____
   - - - - - - - - - - - - - - - -
   I work in a _____.

4. I am an office worker.

   _____
   - - - - - - - - - - - - - - - -
   I work in an _____.

Needs or Wants?

Write **need** or **want** beside each thing.

1. food _____

2. a book _____

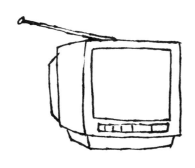

3. a TV _____

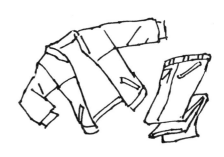

4. clothing _____

5. water _____

6. a dog _____

On a separate paper draw two things people need to live.

Feathers or fur or . . . ?

Write the animal's covering: feathers, fur or hair, scales, shell.

Animal	Covering
cat	
duck	
turtle	
goldfish	

Draw two animals.
Tell a friend about their coverings.

All About Me

Tell about yourself. Finish the story.

_____
- -
My name is _____ .

_____
- - - - - - - - -
I am _____ years old.

_____
- -
I was born in _____ .

_____
- -
I like to _____ .

_____
- -
When I grow up, I want to be a _____ .

Draw a picture of yourself when you are grown up.

Where People Work

Draw four pictures.
Show four different places where people work.

Who wears what?

Write each animal's name beside its covering.
Use the animals shown on this page.

_____   _____
- - - - - - - - - - - - -   - - - - - - - - - - - - -
fur _____   _____

_____
- - - - - - - - - - - - -
shell _____

_____   _____
- - - - - - - - - - - - -   - - - - - - - - - - - - -
feathers _____   _____

_____
- - - - - - - - - - - - -
scales _____

squirrel

cardinal

robin

cat

turtle

fish

Name _____

Math Objective: Use the operations of addition and subtraction to solve problems.

Sample:

Read the story problem carefully. Add or subtract to get the answer.

Miguel returned 4 books to the library. The librarian
showed him 2 new books. Miguel liked 1 of the books.
He told the librarian he wanted to check out the book.
Then Miguel saw 2 more books that he liked.
He checked out these books too.
How many books did Miguel check out?

◯ 8   If you chose 3, you are right.

◯ 4   1 book   the librarian showed him

◯ 3   +2 books   he saw
            _____

◯ 2   3 books   he checked out

Name _____

Try It

Read each story problem.

Add or subtract to answer each question.

1. This week the mail carrier delivered 1 letter to you
   on Monday. Then you got 1 letter on Tuesday,
   1 letter on Friday, and 1 letter on Saturday.
   You did not get a letter on Wedneday.
   How many letters did you get this week?

   ○ 6
   ○ 4
   ○ 5
   ○ 1

2. A TV repair person makes $5.00 for 1 hour of work.
   How much money does he make for 2 hours of work?

   ○ $3.00 + $5.00 = $8.00
   ○ $5.00 + $2.00 = $7.00
   ○ $3.00 + $5.00 = $8.00
   ○ $5.00 + $4.00 = $9.00
   ○ $5.00 + $5.00 = $10.00

3. Hiromi saw 6 ducks in the pond. She saw 4 ducks get out
   of the pond. How many ducks were left in the pond?

   ○ 3
   ○ 2
   ○ 4
   ○ 6

Animals at Work

Draw a line under the action word in each sentence.
Write the action word on the lines.

1. Ants carry pieces of leaves.

2. A bird builds a nest.

3. A squirrel gathers nuts.

4. Beavers cut down small trees.

5. Woodchucks dig tunnels.

6. Woodchucks push dirt out with their back feet.

How Animals Protect Themselves

Read the words in the box.
Write an animal name to complete each sentence.

| bird | chameleon | skunk | turtle |

1. A _____ changes color to protect itself.

2. A _____ smells bad to protect itself.

3. A _____ flies away to protect itself.

4. A _____ hides in its shell to protect itself.

Draw a picture of a turtle hiding in its shell.

Scared Rabbits

Find the three rabbits that want to hide.
Color them so that they are hard to see.

Name _____

Ask a Question

Write the missing question mark ☐ ? ☐ for each question.

Then answer the question.

How many rabbits are there _____
    There are _____ rabbits.

How many ants are there _____
There are _____ ants.

How many turtles are there _____
There are _____ turtles.

Write a question about the fish. Then answer the question.

Begin the question with **How many** and end with a ☐ ? ☐ .

_____

- -

_____

_____

- -

_____

Contractions

Draw a line to match each contraction
with the words it stands for.

he's   I am

she's   he is

I'm   she is

Write a contraction to finish each sentence.

1. Miguel is my brother. When _____ _____ hungry,
   he likes to eat fruit.

2. Maria is my sister. When _____ _____ hungry,
   she likes to drink milk.

3. When _____ _____ hungry, I eat anything that's around!

Find the contraction in sentence 3 that stands for **that is** and circle it.

Action Words

Circle the action word in each sentence.

1. A monkey eats food right off the tree.

2. A butterfly sips nectar from a flower.

3. A frog catches food with its tongue.

4. Ducks float on water.

Choose one of the action words you circled. Write it on the line.

_____

- -

_____

Draw a picture that shows what **your** word means.

Playful Pets

Write words from the box to complete the poem.

be	me	string	things

I have a little puppy

_____

- -

Who loves to play with _____.

He's as fun to play with

_____

- -

As a little pup can _____.

I have a cat named Pumpkin

_____

- -

Who plays with lots of _____.

Like balls, paper, ribbon, yarn,

_____

- -

And she loves to play with _____.

How do some animals work?

Draw a line to match each animal with its work.

honeycomb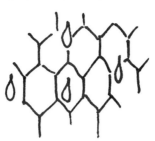

robin

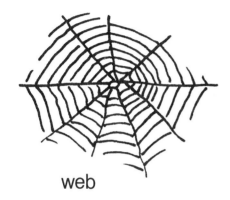

web

spider

tunnel

bee

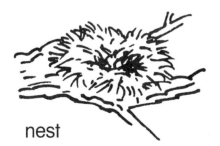

nest

beaver

dam

woodchuck

Reading Objectives: Identify cause and effect relationships. Predict future outcomes.

Read carefully. Think about what happens and why as you answer the questions.

> Sample:
>
> Animals need to protect themselves from other animals. They need to protect themselves because other animals can hurt them. A skunk protects itself by spraying animals. A turtle protects itself from animals by hiding itself in its shell. A rabbit can protect itself from animals by running away very fast.

1. A skunk sprays other animals because

   ○ it needs to protect itself.

   ○ it needs to hide in its shell.

   ○ it wants to help other animals.

   The best choice: It needs to protect itself.

2. What would happen if a rabbit hurt its foot?

   ○ The fur would come off.

   ○ The rabbit would need to see a doctor.

   ○ The rabbit couldn't protect itself.

   The best choice: The rabbit couldn't protect itself.

Name _____

Try It

First read each question. Then read the story.
Answer each question.

Bees make a honeycomb. Then they make honey. They put the honey in the honeycomb. There is always a queen bee. Bees will not make honey if there is not a queen bee.

Beavers live near water. They cut down small trees to build a dam. The dam keeps water from going where it needs to be. Beavers use some of the trees to build a home.

Woodchucks live under the ground. They dig tunnels by using their feet. They dig with their front feet. They push out the dirt with their back feet.

1. Bees make a honeycomb because

   ○ they need air.

   ○ they need a place to put the honey.

   ○ they like to see other bees.

2. What would happen if a woodchuck couldn't build a tunnel?

   ○ It wouldn't have a place to live.

   ○ It would need a coat.

   ○ It would build a dam.

© Scott, Foresman and Company

Sound of Final *s* /z/

Say each picture name.
Draw a circle around the picture if the word ends
with the same sound as *checkers*.

Look at Me!

Draw a picture of an exercise you like to do.

Draw a picture of yourself. Show your lungs.

Action Words

Look at each picture. Then complete the sentence.
Remember to use *is* or *are*.

stretching

jumping

1. He _____ .

2. They _____ .

kicking

playing

3. He _____ .

4. They _____ .

Name _____

Number Stories

Work with a partner. Talk about what happens
in each picture. Then write a number sentence.

_____ + _____ = _____

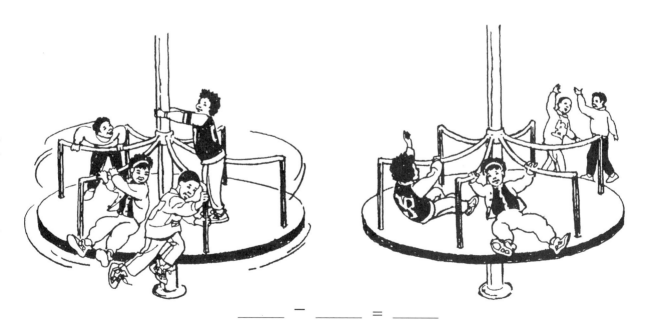

_____ − _____ = _____

What will they do?

Tell what the boy or girl will do.
Use the words in the box to finish each sentence.

| will push | will pull | will swing |
| will ride | will climb | will play |

1. I _____ the slide.

2. I _____ in the
wagon.

3. I _____ the dog in
the wagon.

4. I _____ the
swing.

5. I _____ up high.

6. I _____ with my
friend.

Name _____

Pronouns

Write the word that makes the sentence tell about the picture.

She / He
_____

- - - - - - - - - - - - - - - -

1. _____ can skate.

They / He
_____

- - - - - - - - - - - - - - - -

2. _____ can ride.

We / He
_____

- - - - - - - - - - - - - - - -

3. _____ pushes the door.

you / I
_____

- - - - - - - - - - - - - - - -

4. Will _____ go with me?

He / They
_____

- - - - - - - - - - - - - - - -

5. _____ has a new puppy.

I / She
_____

- - - - - - - - - - - - - - - -

6. _____ hurt herself.

© Scott, Foresman and Company

47

What will we do?

We'll is a short way of saying **We will.**
Read each sentence.

Draw a line to the sentence that means the same.

1. We will go out.   We'll play.

2. We will play.   We'll climb up.

3. We will climb up.   We'll slide down.

4. We will slide down.   We'll have a lot of fun.

5. We will have a lot of fun.   We'll go out.

Draw a picture to show three things we'll do in school today.

Body Parts

Label the parts of the body. Use these words to help you.

| hand | foot | leg | head | arm | ear | eye |

_____

- - - - - - - - - - - - - -

_____

- - - - - - - - - - - - - -

_____

- - - - - - - - - - - - - -

_____

- - - - - - - - - - - - - -

_____

- - - - - - - - - - - - - -

_____

- - - - - - - - - - - - - -

_____

- - - - - - - - - - - - - -

Name _____

Reading Objective: Identify cause and effect relationships.

Read the paragraph. Look in the paragraph for the answer.

Sample:

Making bubbles is fun. You can make big bubbles. You can make very small bubbles too. If bubbles get in your mouth they can make you sick because they are made of soap. Be careful when you make bubbles.

Make sure you keep the bubble wand away from your mouth when you blow bubbles because

○   bubbles are big.

○   bubbles are small.

○   bubbles are made of soap.

○   bubbles can be fun.

The best choice: Bubbles are made of soap.
Bubbles in your mouth can make you sick.

Try It

Read each question. Then read the paragraphs.
Answer each question.

Playing is fun. You can play some games by yourself. You can play some games with 1 friend. You need 2 or more friends to play other games. Everyone has more fun when you take turns.

Playing is good for you too. When you play some games, you get good exercise. Exercise is good for you because it helps you build strong muscles. Since exercise makes you strong, do some running, skipping, and hopping each day as you play. Running, skipping, and hopping are fun and can help you stay healthy.

1. Taking turns is good because

   ○ everyone plays games.

   ○ everyone gets more exercise.

   ○ everyone has more fun.

   ○ everyone wins the game.

2. Running is good for you because it can help

   ○ you eat more.

   ○ you feel tired.

   ○ you stay healthy.

   ○ you win.

Where is it?

Read each phrase. Circle the picture that does not belong.

in the air

on the water

on the ground

 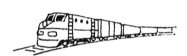 

on the water

on the ground

in the air

Consonant Blend *tr*

Work with a partner. Name what you see in the picture.
Then color the things that begin with the sound of the *tr* blend you hear in *try*.

Using Force

Draw a picture of yourself using force to push or pull something.

Write about your picture.

_____

- -

_____

What do magnets do?

Hold a magnet over each object. See what happens.
Put a check under *Moves* or *Does Not Move*.
Repeat the experiment with other classroom objects.

Object	Moves	Does Not Move
button		
penny		
paper clip		
screw		
barrette		

Pulling or Pushing?

Who is pulling? Who is pushing?
Write **pulling** or **pushing** under each picture.

_____   _____
- - - - - - - - - - - -   - - - - - - - - - - - - - - -
_____   _____

_____   _____
- - - - - - - - - - - -   - - - - - - - - - - - - - - -
_____   _____

On another paper draw a picture of you and your friends having fun.
Show some of you pushing or pulling.

It's a match!

Draw a line to match each picture with the correct word.

 chicken

 mom

 friends

 piñata

 candy

Name _____

At My Party

Write the words that are missing from each sentence.

| will invite | will eat | will play | will go | will break | will clean |

1. I _____ my friends to my party.

2. We _____ a game of tag.

3. We _____ chicken and rice.

4. Who _____ the piñata?

5. My friends _____ home.

6. I _____ our house.

Air, Ground, or Water?

Play Bingo with 3 friends. Put a marker on a picture that matches the phrase on your card.

Math Objective: Use whole number place value.

We can group blocks in rows of 10.
This picture shows 1 row of 10 blocks. There is 1 group of 10.

When there are fewer than 10 blocks, we count them one by one. There are 6 blocks here.

We can show the number 13 as

Sample:

What number is shown here?

○ 20
○ 42
○ 26
○ 24

If you chose 24, you are right! There are 2 groups of 10 = 20.
There are 4 blocks that are not in a group.

Name _____

Try It

1. What number is shown by this group of blocks?

⬜⬜⬜⬜⬜⬜⬜⬜⬜⬜ ⬜⬜⬜
⬜⬜⬜⬜⬜⬜⬜⬜⬜⬜
⬜⬜⬜⬜⬜⬜⬜⬜⬜⬜

- ○ 30
- ○ 13
- ○ 33
- ○ 35

2. Look at this group of blocks.

⬜⬜⬜⬜⬜⬜⬜⬜⬜⬜ ⬜
⬜⬜⬜⬜⬜⬜⬜⬜⬜⬜ ⬜
⬜⬜⬜⬜⬜⬜⬜⬜⬜⬜ ⬜

If we take 2 ⬜⬜⬜⬜⬜⬜⬜⬜⬜⬜ away from the

groups of 10, what number will be left?

- ○ 23
- ○ 13
- ○ 82
- ○ 21

3. Look at this group of blocks.

⬜⬜⬜⬜⬜⬜⬜⬜⬜⬜ ⬜⬜⬜
⬜⬜⬜⬜⬜⬜⬜⬜⬜⬜ ⬜⬜⬜⬜

If we add 1 ⬜ to this group, what number will be shown?

- ○ 25
- ○ 36
- ○ 72
- ○ 28

In the Garden

Finish the words. Use *st* or *str*.
Color the garden.

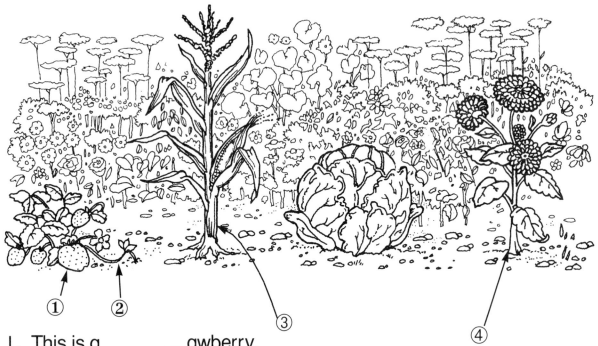

1. This is a _____awberry.

2. This is the _____em

   of the _____awberry plant.

3. This is the _____alk of the corn.

4. This is the _____em of the flower.

What plants do you see in the garden? Make a list.

_____   _____
-     -
_____   _____
-     -
_____   _____
-     -

How many are there?

Complete the sentences. Use *a few* or *a lot of*.

    _____
    - - - - - - - - - - - - - - - - - -
1. Avi has _____ seeds.

    _____
    - - - - - - - - - - - - - - - - - -
2. Magda's plant has _____ leaves.

    _____
    - - - - - - - - - - - - - - - - - -
3. Iris's cactus has _____ flowers.

Draw a plant.

    _____
    - - - - - - - - - - - - - - - - - -
My plant has _____ leaves.

Name _____

Make a Chart

Write the names of plants.

Put the name under the part we eat.

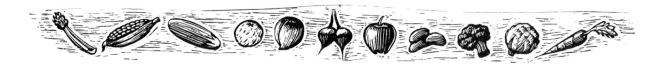

seed	root	stem	leaf	flower	fruit

Draw two plants you eat often. Write what parts you eat.

_____

_____

_____

_____

Which foods are made from grains?

Some of the foods are made from grains.
Circle them.

How many of the foods can you name?

Just think of it!

bread	kitchen	smell

Write a sentence for each picture.

Add a word from the box to "Think of the _____."

_____

- -

_____

_____

- -

_____

_____

- -

_____

What's happening?

Read the sentences.

Write an action word to complete each sentence.

eating	baking	shining	sleeping

1. The seed is _____ in the ground.

2. The sun is _____ on the earth.

3. The baker is _____ the bread.

4. The people are _____ the bread.

Draw a picture of little sprouts coming up from the ground.

What do they do?

Read each question.
Circle the correct answer.

1. What does the farmer do? The farmer _____.

   tills the soil   kneads the flour

2. What does the harvester do? The harvester _____.

   cuts the wheat   shines down on the earth

3. What does the miller do? The miller _____.

   bakes the bread   grinds the grain

4. What does the storekeeper do? The storekeeper _____.

   loads the grain   sells us flour

5. What does the baker do? The baker _____.

   bakes the bread   hopes for rain

6. What do the children do? The children _____.

   eat the bread   load the truck

Plant Puzzles

Use words from the box to complete each puzzle.

stem	fruit	root	seeds	leaves	grain

Across →
barley and oats

Down ↓
apples and bananas

Across →
We eat this part
of a carrot.

Down ↓
We eat this
part of celery.

Across →
We eat this part
of cabbage.

Down ↓
We eat this
part of corn.

Name _____

Reading Objectives: Determine the meaning of words in a variety of texts.
Analyze information in order to make conclusions.

Sample:

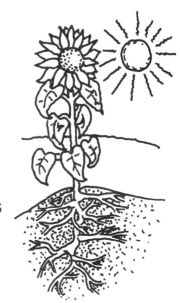

A plant is a living thing. It needs food and water. It gets food and water in different ways. Leaves use the light from the sun to make food. Roots get water from under the ground. They carry the water to stems and other parts of the plant. The water helps the plant grow.

1. In this story *roots* are
   ○ the part of the plant under the ground.
   ○ the fruit of the plant.
   ○ the part of the plant next to the leaves.
   ○ the part of the plant over the stems.
   Look in the same sentence with the word *roots.* Do you see the answer?
   The best choice: the part of the plant under the ground.

2. A plant needs food and water
   ○ to get light.
   ○ to sleep.
   ○ to live.
   ○ to move.
   Look at the sentence before the sentence with the words *food* and *water.* Plants are living things. Do you see the answer? Living comes from the verb to live.
   The best choice: to live.

Try It

Read the questions and possible answers. Then read the story. Look for clues in the story to help you.

We have lots of bread at our house. Sometimes my mother has to tell my little brother to eat the bread on his plate. She tells him "bread is for eating!" Then she tells him how we get bread.

Bread starts as a seed in the ground. The seed sleeps. Then the rain and sun wake it up. Soon the seed comes up through the soil. The farmer tills the soil. The farmer waits for the seed to grow into a grain plant. The grain plant goes to the miller who grinds the grain into flour. The baker and the cook use the flour to make bread.

My little brother wants to eat the bread now. He thinks of all the people that made the grain into bread.

1. In the story, a mill is a place where the workers
   ○ till soil.
   ○ sing songs.
   ○ grow grain.
   ○ grind grain.

2. How do you think the little boy feels at the end of the story?
   ○ hungry
   ○ happy to have bread
   ○ sleepy
   ○ sad for the world

Where We Buy Food

Circle the foods we can buy at a bakery.

Circle the foods we can buy from an ice cream truck.

Circle the foods we can buy at a farmers' market.

Draw two foods you buy at a grocery store or supermarket. Tell what they are.

_____   _____

-        -

_____   _____

What do you enjoy?

Draw a picture. Show what you would <u>enjoy seeing</u> on a farm.

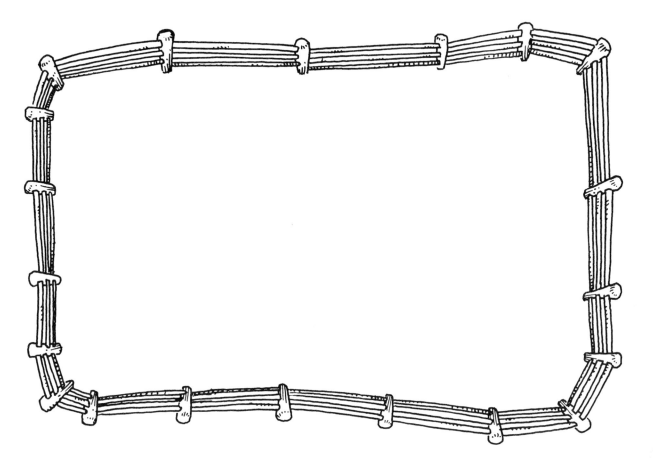

Next, draw a picture of three things you would <u>enjoy buying</u> at a farm stand. Draw three fruits or vegetables.

Special Names

These are special names of people.
Write each name with a capital letter.

_____
- -

tomás _____

_____
- -

teiko _____

_____
- -

annie _____

_____
- -

ken _____

These are special names of places.
Write each name with a capital letter.

_____
- -

japan _____

_____
- -

mexico _____

_____
- -

africa _____

_____
- -

korea _____

What do they say?

Each person is asking to buy something.
Put a check next to the sentence that tells what he
or she is saying.

At the Hot Dog Stand

_____ I'd like a hot dog, please.

_____ Where is the supermarket?

At the Farm Stand

_____ I'd like some apples, please.

_____ I'd like to live on a farm.

At the Bakery

_____ The bakery smells good.

_____ I'd like some bread, please.

At the Ice Cream Truck

_____ I'd like some ice cream, please.

_____ Ice cream is cold.

How many will you get?

Draw the correct number of things.

four bananas	one carrot
six apples	two cabbages
nine tomatoes	three ice cream cones

The Pet Belongs to —

Look at each picture. Find the person's name.
Use *'s* to show who the pet in the picture belongs to.

_____
- -
_____ bird

_____
- -
_____ dog

_____
- -
_____ fish

_____
- -
_____ cat

On a separate paper draw a picture of you and a pet. Make a label for your picture here.

_____
- -
_____

Name _____

All About Me

Write *me* on the line in each sentence. Read the sentences to a friend.

1. Is this for ⎯⎯⎯⎯⎯?

2. Bring ⎯⎯⎯⎯⎯ your paper.

3. The sun made ⎯⎯⎯⎯⎯ hot.

4. Can you see ⎯⎯⎯⎯⎯?

5. I want you to go with ⎯⎯⎯⎯⎯.

6. Mom will help ⎯⎯⎯⎯⎯.

Write a sentence about yourself. Use the word *me*.

_____

_____

Where will you go?

Look at the words in the box. Write the words next to the place where you buy them. Some words can go in more than one place.

corn	fish	cake	cocoa	strawberries
bread	tomatoes	bananas	cookies

bakery

farmers' market

supermarket

Name _____

Math Objectives: Use the operations of addition, subtraction, multiplication, and division to solve problems.

Sample:

1. Ivan and Jaime went to the grocery store. They saw bananas. Each group of bananas is a bunch. First, count how many bunches of bananas there are. Then, count how many bananas are in each bunch.

   How many bananas are there in all?

   ○ 15

   ○ 3

   ○ 10

   ○ 25

   Did you choose 15? You're right! There are 3 bunches of bananas.

   There are 5 bananas in each bunch.
   So, we can say 5 +5 + 5 = 15. Or, we can say 3 x 5 =15.

2. Nalin and Van went to the farm stand. Each girl had a bag. They saw 12 apples. They wanted to make equal shares for 2 bags. How many apples would each girl buy?

   ○ 12

   ○ 3

   ○ 4

   ○ 6

   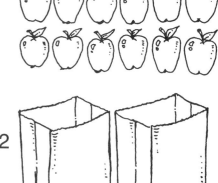

   Did you choose 6? You're right! There are 12 apples in all. There are 2 girls. So, there would be 6 apples for each girl. We can say that there are 2 groups of 6 in 12.

Try It

1. Marcus saw an ice cream truck on the street. He wanted to buy some ice cream bars. Count how many groups of ice cream bars there are. Count how many bars are in each group. How many ice cream bars did Marcus see in all?

- ○ 1
- ○ 3
- ○ 3 + 3 + 3 = 9
- ○ 4 x 3 = 12

2. Patricia has 6 apples. She wants to share the apples with 2 friends. She wants to make equal shares. How many apples will each of the 3 friends get?

- ○ 4
- ○ 6
- ○ 2
- ○ 3

3. Laura had 60¢. She gave Juan 30¢. How much money does Laura have left?

- ○ 90¢
- ○ 30¢
- ○ 60¢
- ○ 18¢

4. Maria wants to buy 2 tacos. They cost 45¢ each. How much will she spend?

- ○ 90¢
- ○ 25¢
- ○ 80¢
- ○ 45¢

Name _____

A Wish on a Star

Draw your wish inside the star.
Write what your wish is on the line.

_____

- -

_____

Name _____

Choose the right/write word.

The words in dark type sound the same when you say them out loud. Which one makes sense in the sentence? Write that word on the line.

1. The **son/sun** lights the earth.   _____

2. We sleep at **night/knight.**   _____

3. The moon has **no/know** water.   _____

4. **Write/Right** a question about the moon.   _____

Now use the words that you didn't write to finish this poem.

_____

The king had a _____,

_____

A brave, handsome _____.

_____

He didn't _____ much,

_____

But he knew wrong from _____.

Compound Words

Draw a line to match each sentence to its picture.

1. **Sunlight** melts the ice cube.

a.

2. Jo wears **sunglasses** on sunny days.

b.

3. **Sunrise** is the beginning of the day.

c.

4. Tomás does not want a **sunburn**.

d.

5. Today is **Sunday**.

e.

Name _____

It's about time!

Use the right word to measure time.
Write the word from the box that makes
the most sense in the sentence.

days	weeks	months	years

1. You are about eight _____ old.

2. You go to school five _____ a week.

3. Summer vacation is almost three _____ long.

4. Winter break lasts for two _____.

Write a sentence that tells one thing you learned about time.

_____

_____

Today and Long Ago

Change the underlined word to show that
the action happened in the past.
Use the new word to complete the sentence.

Today we <u>write</u> with words.

_____

- - - - - - - - - - - - - - - - - - - -

Long ago people _____

with pictures.

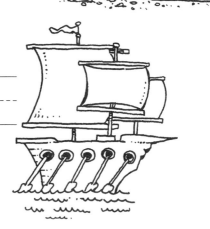

Today we <u>watch</u> sports on T.V.

_____

- - - - - - - - - - - - - - - - - - - -

Long ago people _____

sports in the Colisseum.

Today we <u>find</u> new worlds in space.

_____

- - - - - - - - - - - - - - - - - - - -

Long ago people _____

new worlds across the ocean.

Name _____

Words That Compare

Look for the **-er** ending.
If the sentence has a word that compares,
write the word on the line.

1. The water is dark. _____

2. My dog is darker than the water. _____

3. The sky is wide. _____

4. The sky is wider than the river. _____

5. A turtle is slow. _____

6. A turtle is slower than a rabbit. _____

Choose one of the sentences that compares.
Write the two things that are compared.

_____   _____

It's like this.

Tell what is being compared in each sentence.

1. The sky is like a clock, telling us whether it is night or day.

   _____
   _

   The sky is being compared to a _____.

2. The Big Dipper is like a ladle that could dip a drink out of the sea.

   _____
   _

   The Big Dipper is being compared to a _____.

3. The sun hangs in the sky like a big golden plate.

   _____
   _

   The sun is being compared to a _____.

Describe the moon by comparing it to something else.

   _____
   _

The moon is like a _____.

Name _____

Vocabulary Assessment

Use the words in the box to complete each activity.

hour	day	night	earth	month	year	light	heat

1. Find the words that describe time. Write them on
   the blanks from the longest time to the shortest.

_____

_____

_____

_____

_____

2. Write the words that have opposite meanings.

_____

_____ is the opposite of dark.

_____

_____ is the opposite of day.

3. Move the letters around to write two words from
   the box.

_____

thear _____

_____

thae _____

Name _____

Math Objectives: Demonstrate an understanding of measurement concepts.
Demonstrate an understanding of probabilities and statistics.

Sample:

1. Think about putting 4 moons and 1 sun in a bag.
   If you picked 1 object out of the bag, which object
   would you more likely pick?

   ○ the sun
   ○ the moon

   If you picked the moon, you're right! There are
   more moons than suns, so you are more likely
   to pick the moon.

2. Use the graph to answer the question.

Stories Read By 2nd Graders in 1 Month					
Elena					
Ana					
Carlos					
	1	2	3	4	5

Who read the most stories in 1 month?
○ Carlos and Elena
○ Elena
○ Carlos
○ Ana and Carlos

Elena is the right answer! She read 5 stories
which is 1 story more than Carlos read.

Name _____

Try It

1. What time is it?
   ○ 6:15
   ○ 4:30
   ○ 11:30
   ○ 3:30

2. Use the graph to answer the question.
   On which day was the most homework done?

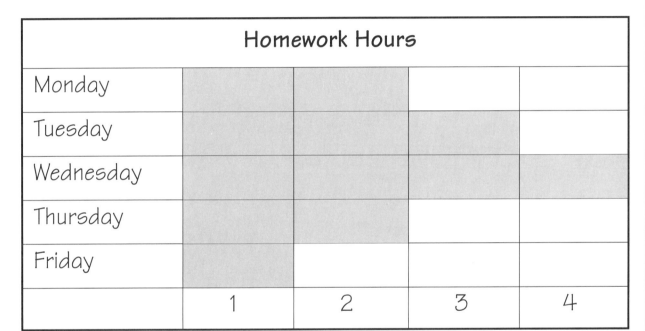

Homework Hours			
Monday			
Tuesday			
Wednesday			
Thursday			
Friday			
	1	2	3	4

   ○ Monday
   ○ Tuesday
   ○ Wednesday
   ○ Thursday

3. Think about putting 3 stars and 9 moons in a bag.
   If you picked 1 object out of the bag, which object
   would you more likely pick?

   ○ the star
   ○ the moon

Name _____

Long Ago and Today

Think about what people used long ago. Find what
people use to do the same things today. Draw lines
to match the pictures from long ago to the pictures of today.

Long Ago   **Today**

1.

horse

stove

2.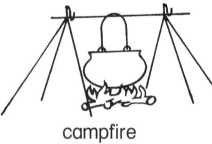

campfire

light bulb

3.

candle

car

Choose 1 pair of pictures. Write about what these
things helped people do long ago and today.

_____

- -

_____

- -

_____

Telling Why

Complete the following sentences. Use some of the words in the box.

to learn English	to buy bread	to protect itself
to wash the dishes	to tell time	to stay healthy

People use clocks _____ _____.

A skunk sprays a bad smell _____ _____.

People go to a bakery _____ _____.

Exercise _____ _____.

You come to school _____ _____.

Work with a partner. Write your own sentence telling why.

_____

_____.

A Year With the Pilgrims

Read the sentences.
Tell what happened in the correct time order.

Write *1* before what happened first.

Write *2* before what happened second.

Write *3* before what happened third.

Write *4* before what happened last.

_____ In the spring, the Indians helped the Pilgrims plant food.

_____ Many Pilgrims died during their first winter in North America.

_____ The Pilgrims and the Indians shared the first Thanksgiving in the fall.

_____ A lot of food crops grew in the summer.

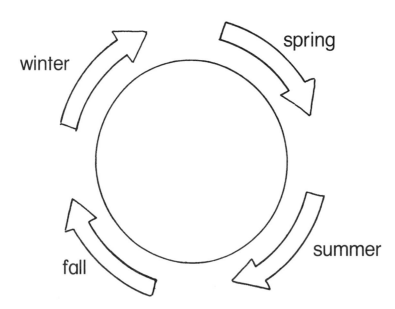

Using Calendars

Look at the calendar pages. Fill in the blanks.
Use the words in the box.

first second third fourth fifth

_____

Martin Luther King Day is on the _____ Monday in January.

New Year's Day is on the _____ day of January.

Mother's Day is on the _____ Sunday of May.

Cinco de Mayo is on the _____ day of May.

Thanksgiving is on the _____ Thursday in November.

Name _____

How Many? Which?

Use the pictures to count how many.
Write your answer.

1. How many flags do you see? _____

2. How many pumpkins do you see? _____

Look at the calendar pages below.
Write the day on which the holiday comes.

1. On which day is Columbus Day celebrated? _____

2. On which day is Halloween celebrated? _____

October

Sunday	Monday	Tuesday	Wednesday	Thursday	Friday	Saturday
			1	2	3	4
5	6	7	8	9	10	11
12	Columbus Day 13	14	15	16	17	18
19	20	21	22	23	24	25
26	27	28	29	30	Halloween 31	

My Favorite Holiday

Write the name of your favorite holiday on the line below.

1. My favorite holiday is _____.

2. Here is a picture of me having fun on that holiday.

3. On that holiday I like to _____.

4. The holiday I'd like to learn more about is _____.

Using Verbs

Fill in the blanks with different action words to complete the story.

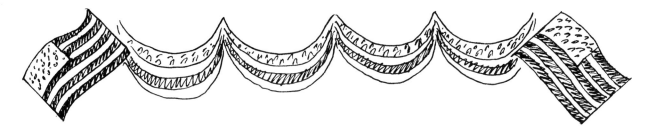

Today is Independence Day. In the afternoon, my

_____

mom _____ me some money. Then

_____

we _____ to the store. We

_____ a lot of fruit. She

_____ the fruit on a plate. Then she

_____ it up. At night, some family and

friends _____ to our house. We

_____ outside. We _____

firecrackers.

Vocabulary Assessment

_____

- -

_____ were the first people in North America.

_____

- -

Next, the _____ people came. They built

_____

- -

_____ in many places.

_____

- -

Later, the _____ came. The first Thanksgiving was

_____

- -

celebrated by the _____ and the

_____

- -

_____ .

_____

- -

Thanksgiving was celebrated long ago. That _____

_____

- -

is still celebrated _____ . If you look at the month

_____

- -

of November on a _____ , you will see the day

marked.

Reading Objective: Summarize a variety of texts.

Think about all the ideas in the paragraph. Then think about the most important idea. A summary has the most important ideas.

Sample:

Day and night happen at different times around the world. The earth keeps turning around and around. It takes 24 hours or one day for the earth to turn one time. The sun lights different parts of the earth because the earth keeps turning. The part of the earth that faces the sun has day. It is light during the day. The part of the earth that doesn't face the sun has night. It is dark at night. When it is dark at your house it will be light in another part of the world.

What is the best summary of this paragraph?

○ The earth turns.

○ There are 24 hours in one day.

○ The sun and earth work together to make day and night happen at different times around the world.

○ It is light during the day.

The most important idea in the paragraph is that the sun and earth make day and night. The best choice: The sun and earth work together to make day and night happen at different times around the world.

Name _____

Try It

Look at the questions. Then read the story.
Answer the questions.

Long ago people all over the world learned about time. People in Egypt looked at the sky during the day. They watched the sun. They looked at the sky at night. They watched the moon. They made calendars. On the calendars, they showed that a year was about 365 days. They showed that a month was about 30 days.

People in Central America watched the sun and the moon. They made calendars that looked different from the Egyptian calendars, but the Central American calendars had about 365 days in a year too.

Today people in the United States use a calendar that has about 365 days in a year and about 30 days in a month.

1. What is the best summary of the first paragraph?
   ○ People in Egypt looked at the moon.
   ○ There are about 365 days in a year.
   ○ People in Egypt made a calendar with about 365 days in a year and about 30 days in a month.
   ○ People all over the world learned about time.

2. What is the best summary of this story?
   ○ A month has 30 days.
   ○ People from long ago and today have learned the same things about time.
   ○ People make calendars.
   ○ People in Egypt watched the sun and the moon.

Describe it.

Draw a line from the picture to the word or words that describe it.

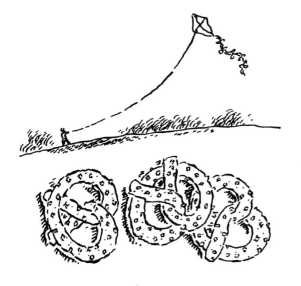

small

moving

in the air

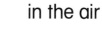

very large

salty

wet

Capitals

Read each sentence. On the lines, write the
words that should be capitalized.

1. The atlantic ocean is east of north america.

_____   _____

_____   _____

_____   _____

_____   _____

_____   _____

2. illinois is across the mississippi river from missouri.

_____   _____

_____   _____

_____   _____

_____   _____

_____   _____

3. The pacific ocean is west of north and south America.

_____   _____

_____   _____

_____   _____

_____   _____

_____   _____

Work with a partner to write a sentence about a body
of water near your home.

_____

_____

_____

Name _____

How much?

Complete the sentences. Use **a little** or **a lot of**.

_____
- -
1. There is _____ water in
   the Atlantic Ocean.

_____
- -
2. The dishes still have _____ water
   on them.

_____
- -
3. It takes _____ water to make
   a lake.

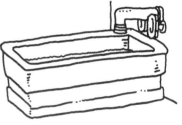

_____
- -
4. The tub has _____ water in it.

Now draw something from your house that holds a lot of water and
something that holds a little water. Write what they are.

_____   _____
- - - - - - - - - - - - - - - - - - -   - - - - - - - - - - - - - - - - - - -
_____   _____

Where's the long *a*?

Listen as your teacher reads these sentences.
Listen for the word with the long *a* sound.
Write the word on the line.

1. Does your state have many bodies of water?

   _____

   -

   _____

2. We should not waste water.

   _____

   -

   _____

3. In some countries, it does not rain for weeks or months.

   _____

   -

   _____

4. It is sad to see a lake that has gone dry.

   _____

   -

   _____

5. If we don't start to save water now, we won't have it tomorrow.

   _____

   -

   _____

What did they do?

Complete each sentence.
Write the word that contains the short *u* sound.

lunch / dinner

_____

- -

1. Henry and Mudge had hot dogs for _____ .

gulp / bite

_____

- -

2. Mudge ate his hot dogs in one _____ .

help / fun

_____

- -

3. Henry had _____ building a sand castle.

stuck / placed

_____

- -

4. Henry's father _____ a rubber lobster on
the tower.

sand / sun

_____

- -

5. Mudge fell asleep in the _____ .

ran / jumped

_____

- -

6. Mudge _____ into the waves to save the
lobster.

Henry's Things

Write **'s** on the blanks to show things that belong to Henry.
Then draw a picture of each thing that belongs to Henry.

——
- - - - - - -
Henry_____ father

——
- - - - - - -
Henry_____ dog, Mudge

——
- - - - - - -
Henry_____ castle

——
- - - - - - -
Henry_____ cherry sno-cone

Long and Short *i*

Listen as your teacher reads each sentence.
Draw a line under the word with the long *i* sound.
Draw a circle around the word with the short *i* sound.

1. Grandma sips her iced tea on the porch.

2. We like to listen to her stories.

3. She told us a fine story about big steamboats.

4. Grandma's grandpa was a riverboat pilot.

5. His boat had paddle wheels on the sides.

6. One time the boat got stuck in the mud.

7. It took twenty mules to slide the boat off of the mud.

8. Life on the river wasn't easy!

Vocabulary Assessment

Draw lines to match the words on the left
with the phrases on the right.

water	very large body of water that is salty
desert	smaller than an ocean, larger than a pond
ocean	body of water that moves
dry	what oceans, ponds, and rivers have
lake	place that gets very little rain
pond	opposite of wet
river	smallest body of water in the list

Now look at the word search.
Find the words that are listed on the left above and circle them.

j	l	u	g	w	y	p	o	n	d
z	p	e	h	a	s	i	c	e	r
u	b	l	q	t	o	n	u	v	y
o	d	o	c	e	a	n	l	a	r
f	e	e	f	r	y	w	a	z	u
e	s	r	o	s	d	g	k	j	d
t	e	b	t	r	i	v	e	r	d
n	r	a	i	n	s	q	u	a	r
s	t	y	x	s	t	r	e	a	m

Reading Objective: Recognize statements that are fact or non-fact.

Sample:

People use water for a lot of things. They use it for drinking, fishing, swimming, washing, and watering plants. Families use water for cooking too. Some foods like beans need to be cooked in water. It would be very hard to live in a world without water.

A fact is always true. Which sentence is a FACT?

○ Swimming is fun.

○ Fishing is good for you.

○ Water is used for a lot of things.

○ All people like to water plants.

Look at the paragraph. Three sentences are about what some people think, but which sentence is always true?
The best choice: Water is used for a lot of things.

Try It

Look at the questions. Then read the story. Answer the questions.

We can find bodies of water in a lot of places. A pond is a small body of water. It has land on all sides. You can see a friend who is on the opposite side from you because the area is small. Some people use ponds for fishing.

Most of the time a lake is larger than a pond. A lake has land on all sides too. Some people use lakes for boating, swimming, and fishing.

A river is a moving body of water. Rivers flow into lakes, oceans, or other rivers. Some people use rivers for boating and fishing.

An ocean is the largest body of water. It is salty too. Some people use oceans for fishing and for traveling from one country to another country.

1. Which sentence is a FACT that tells about the ocean?

   ○ An ocean is a small body of water.

   ○ Ocean water is salty.

   ○ Ocean water is warm.

   ○ All people like to swim in the ocean.

2. Which sentence is not a FACT from the story?

   ○ Rivers flow into oceans.

   ○ Salt water fish are big.

   ○ People use rivers for fishing.

   ○ Ponds have land on all sides.

Stormy Weather

Complete the sentences that tell about weather.
Use the words from the box.

| rainbow | drizzle | storm | puddles | clouds |

_____

First, _____ form in the sky.

_____

Next, the rain comes down in a light _____.

_____

Then the rain comes down harder, and a _____ begins.

_____

The hard rain makes _____ on the sidewalk.

_____

Finally, the rain stops and a _____ comes out.

Rainy Day

Use the words in the box to label the things that help
keep the boy dry.
Then color the picture.

raincoat	umbrella	boots

Weather Words

Write the correct word for each sentence.

cloud	cloudy	wind	windy	rain	rainy

_____

- -

We won't see the sun all day. It will be a _____ day.

_____

- -

Take your umbrella. The day will be _____ too.

_____

- - - - - - - - - - - - - - - - - - - -

The flag waves in the _____.

_____

- - - - - - - - - - - - - - - - - - - -

We need a _____ day to fly my big kite.

_____

- - - - - - - - - - - - - - - - - - - -

One white _____ floats in the sky.

_____

- -

Our poor garden needs _____ soon.

What a Question

Add a period to the end of each sentence that tells something.
Add a question mark to the end of each sentence that asks a question.
Circle the word that told you the sentence asks a question.

1. What do you see on the cup _____

2. Water in the air is called water vapor_____

3. Cool water vapor in the air changes to drops of water _____

4. What does a puddle look like after the rain _____

5. How does a puddle look after it has been in the sun _____

6. I think it will rain today _____

7. Where did you fill the cup with ice water _____

From and To

Read each sentence.

Use the words **from** and **to** to decide which way the action goes.

Then circle the picture that goes with the sentence.

The dog runs from the girl to the boy.

The gift was from Uncle Frank to Alexis.

We ran from the swings to the slide.

We are in school from eight o'clock to two o'clock.

I will be gone from Tuesday to Saturday.

January						
S	M	T	W	T	F	S
	1	2	3	4	5	6	7
8	9	X̶	X̶	X̶	X̶	X̶
15	16	17	18	19	20	21
22	23	24	25	26	27	28
29	30	31				

January						
S	M	T	W	T	F	S
	1	2	3	4	5	6	7
8	9	10	11	12	13	X̶
X̶	X̶	X̶	18	19	20	21
22	23	24	25	26	27	28
29	30	31				

More or Less

Write the word that correctly finishes each sentence.

dry   drier

_____

- -

1. A desert is _____ than a lake.

windy   windier

_____

- -

2. It's even _____ today than it was yesterday!

wet   wetter

_____

- -

3. The rain got you all _____ .

hot   hotter

_____

- -

4. Yesterday, Chicago was _____ than Dallas.

rainy   rainier

_____

- -

5. This April is _____ than last April.

cold   colder

_____

- -

6. Snow is _____ than rain.

Water, Water, Everywhere

Think of four different ways you use water.
Write them on the lines.

1. _____

2. _____

3. _____

4. _____

Write about a funny thing that happened when you
or someone you know was using water.

_____

_____

_____

_____

Now draw a picture of what you just wrote about.

Name _____

Vocabulary Assessment

Match each picture with the word that describes it.

inch

bath

rainbow

water

sun

raindrop

Math Objectives: Estimate solutions to a problem. Determine solutions to solve a problem. Determine if a solution is reasonable.

Sample:

1. Look at the answer choices. Read the problem. Make a guess. See if your answer makes sense. When you make a careful guess, you are making an estimate.

   Adriana went to the store to buy a calendar for herself and one for her friend. One costs $8. The other costs $11. If she buys both calendars, about how much is the sum?

   $8 + $11 =

   ○ more than $20

   ○ less than $20

   If you said less than $20, you're right! $8 + $11 = $19.

2. Read the problem. What estimate makes the most sense? Lee went to bed early one night. He slept well. He woke up the next morning and got ready for school. How many hours did Lee sleep?

   ○ 4 hours
   ○ 10 hours
   ○ 18 hours
   ○ 24 hours

If you said 10 hours, you're right! Most people sleep about 8 hours a night. If Lee went to bed early, he probably slept a little more than 8 hours.

3. Add or subtract to solve the problem.
Dora has 8 plants. She watered 3 plants. Then her father asked her to come in the house to help him set the table for dinner. How many plants did Dora have left to water?

   ○ 4
   ○ 11
   ○ 3
   ○ 5

If you said 5, you're right.
8 − 3 = 5.

Try It

1. Make a guess about the answer.
   See if the answer makes sense.

   About how much is the sum?

   $24 + 19 =$

   ○ more than 40
   ○ less than 40

2. What estimate makes the most sense? If it rained all
   during the day on Saturday, how long did it rain?
   ○ 3 hours
   ○ 8 hours
   ○ 50 hours
   ○ 60 hours

3. Add or subtract to solve the problem.
   It rained for 9 hours. Then it rained for 6 more hours.
   How many hours did it rain in all?
   ○ 4
   ○ 14
   ○ 3
   ○ 15

Word Log

These are words that I want to learn to use.

Word Log

These are words that I want to learn to use.

Word Log

These are words that I want to learn to use.